ISBN 978-1-330-18324-3
PIBN 10046743

1 MONTH OF
FREE
READING

at

www.ForgottenBooks.com

By purchasing this book you are eligible for one month membership to ForgottenBooks.com, giving you unlimited access to our entire collection of over 1,000,000 titles via our web site and mobile apps.

To claim your free month visit:
www.forgottenbooks.com/free46743

English
Français
Deutsche
Italiano
Español
Português

www.forgottenbooks.com

Mythology Photography **Fiction**
Fishing Christianity **Art** Cooking
Essays Buddhism Freemasonry
Medicine **Biology** Music **Ancient
Egypt** Evolution Carpentry Physics
Dance Geology **Mathematics** Fitness
Shakespeare **Folklore** Yoga Marketing
Confidence Immortality Biographies
Poetry **Psychology** Witchcraft
Electronics Chemistry History **Law**
Accounting **Philosophy** Anthropology
Alchemy Drama Quantum Mechanics
Atheism Sexual Health **Ancient History**
Entrepreneurship Languages Sport
Paleontology Needlework Islam
Metaphysics Investment Archaeology
Parenting Statistics Criminology
Motivational

Ten Masterpieces

beautiful gift volumes

exquisitely bound in
Red Silk Cloth and Mottled Board
printed in two colors

The Progress Series

On The Heights
by C. D. LARSON

The Hidden Secret
by C. D. LARSON

The Great Within
by C D. LARSON

Mastery of Fate
by C. D. LARSON

Poise and Power
by C. D. LARSON

Mastery of Self
by C. D. LARSON

As A Man Thinketh
by JAMES ALLEN

The Greatest Thing In The World
by HENRY DRUMMOND

The Great Stone Face
by NATHANIEL HAWTHORNE

Murad The Unlucky
by MARIA EDGEWORTH

Price — postage paid — 50c each
Ten volumes in a box, postage paid—$5.00

Published by

THE PROGRESS COMPANY

On The Heights

BY

CHRISTIAN D. LARSON

Editor of

ETERNAL PROGRESS

AND

THE COSMIC WORLD

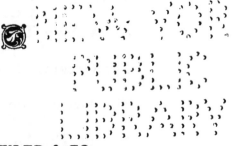

L. N. FOWLER & CO.
7, Imperial Arcade, Ludgate Circus
LONDON, E. C.

1908
THE PROGRESS COMPANY
CHICAGO

Copyright, 1908

BY

THE PROGRESS COMPANY

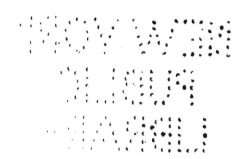

Walking With God.

My God, my Father, I am Thine;
Thy heavenly riches all are mine;
Thy spirit reigns within my heart,
From Thee my soul can not depart.

Wher'er I go, I walk with Thee,
Upon my path, Thou leadest me;
In all my ways Thou art my guide,
For Thou art ever at my side.

I live in Thee, and think Thy thought,
In every deed Thy power is sought,
I consecrate my life to Thee,
And all is ever well with me.

On The Heights

WHEN we transcend the world of things and begin to live on the borderland of the splendor and immensity of the cosmic world, we discover that the vision of the soul was true. Those lofty realms that we have dreamed of so often and so long are dreams no more; we find those realms to be real, the prophetic visions of our sublime moments are fulfilled, and our joy is great beyond measure.

The soul no longer dwells in the limitations of personal form, but is awakened to the glory and magnificence of its own divine existence.

The mind is illumined by the light of the great eternal sun, and the body becomes the consecrated temple of the spirit. The ills of life take flight, the imperfect passes away, and we find ourselves in a new heaven and a new earth.

Beautiful beyond description is the new life we have now begun to live; every moment is an eternity of bliss, and to live—simply to live—that is sufficient. We can ask for nothing more; we have received everything that the heart can wish for; we are in that higher world where every prayer is answered, where every desire is granted, where every need is abundantly supplied; we are ON THE HEIGHTS, where God is closer than breathing, nearer than hands and feet.

It is the world beautiful, the world into which the Christ ascended when his face did shine as the sun and his garment became white as the light. "And where I am there ye shall be also." The gates are ajar; we may enter today and dwell therein while still in personal form. It is the sublime world of the life eternal, and when we enter that life, it is then we begin to live.

To enter this beautiful world is to find the joy everlasting, the peace that passeth understanding, the harmony that is endless symphonies divine; and as the soul is touched by these symphonies of heaven, we mount upon the wings of the spirit and soar to empyrian heights.

The veil of mystery is taken away, we meet Him face to face, and the great secret is revealed. "Eye hath not seen, nor ear heard, neither hath it entered into the heart of man what God has prepared for them that love Him;" but now we are ON THE HEIGHTS, far beyond the life of mere man, and we have seen what eternity has in store. The supreme significance of life is revealed, and when we think that this is life—our own eternal life—our hearts are filled with unbounded thanksgiving.

Henceforth we have something to live for; existence itself has become an endless inspiration; everything is animated with a great divine purpose; nothing is in vain; all is beautiful and all is good. We have entered into the realization of the great truth that "God's in his heaven, all's right with the world," and again our hearts are filled with unbounded thanksgiving.

The world into which we have ascended is God's own world; it is the real world, the true world, the world of the spirit where all things are created in the likeness of God. Therefore, in that world, all is right and all is well. It is the world of spiritual existence, where the eye is too pure to see anything but that which is good, where the mind is too luminous to know anything but that which is truth, where the body is too wholesome to feel anything but that which is health and purity. It is the world of complete emancipation—

the great inheritance that eternity holds in store for man.

But this inheritance is not simply for the eternities that are to be; it is for all eternities—the eternity that now is and the eternities that are to be. It is the kingdom of heaven that is now at hand, the kingdom that shall evermore be at hand, and we may enter its many mansions when we begin to live ON THE HEIGHTS.

WHEN we ascend to the heights and begin to live in the luminous splendor of the cosmic, our spiritual vision is opened to the great truth that "there is another and a better world." This better world is the home of the soul, the kingdom of the spirit, the celestial city on high. It is not a far away place but a realm of the spirit here and now. Its jasper walls, its golden streets and its crystal spires—all may be found on the shining shores of the great within.

That better world is not simply for some future state of being; it is the home of the soul to-day, and when the soul is awakened to the splendor and beauty of its own sublime existence, we shall find that this spiritual kingdom is our home now. Though we may manifest ourselves in the world of things, we are living in the world of the spirit, and to know that we are living in the spirit—that indeed is life.

To live ON THE HEIGHTS is to be in harmony with all the world. In this transcendent realm we are in spiritual touch with the divine side of every living creature. We see all things as they are in the true reality of being, and in the light of this reality all is beautiful and all is well. There are no imperfections ON THE HEIGHTS; nothing to censure, nothing to condemn; love is the law of life, and to love all things at all times is a joy that cannot be measured.

In this higher world, to live is to love, and since life is boundless, love is boundless; therefore to love is to love everybody. The love that is boundless goes to all things, encircles all things and loves all things. We feel its exquisite tenderness the very moment we are on the verge of the heights, and with the prophets of other days, we declare from the very depth of the heart, it is good to be here. We are treading upon holy ground and we know that the kingdom is at hand.

When we enter the kingdom we learn the beautiful secret of love; we then understand those loving words of the Christ, "Come unto me and I will give you rest;" for the soul abides forever in the arms of Infinite

Love, and this is the rest that is in store. Well may the prophet proclaim in language divine, "There is another and a better world."

This better world is the secret places of the Most High; that inner state of divine being where we enter into oneness with the Infinite, and meet Him face to face. It is the true house of prayer, the temple of God, the sacred tabernacle of the soul. To enter therein is to walk with God—to feel that He protects us and keeps us, and to know that He is with us always, even unto the end of the world.

To dwell in the secret places of the Most High is to live under the guidance of the Almighty; therefore no ill can befall us; we cannot go wrong;

we are led by the spirit and the spirit invariably leads towards the heights. What we may desire to know we shall be given the wisdom to know; what we may desire to do we shall be given the power to do, because God is with us, and with God all things are possible.

To be led by the spirit is to be led into greater and greater good always; the spirit leads away from the ills of life into the greater joys of life; the ways of the spirit are ways of pleasantness and all her paths are peace; and the ways of the spirit shall be our ways when we begin to live ON THE HEIGHTS.

THE supreme goal of human life is cosmic consciousness; to live in the cosmic world—the sublime world of the spirit—this is the dearest desire of every awakened soul. It is in cosmic consciousness that the fulness of life, and the divine sweetness of life is realized; and it is in the cosmic that the soul finds the great climax of every joy in the world.

It is cosmic consciousness that reveals everything that is lofty and beautiful, everything that is pure and perfect, everything that is created in the likeness of the Most High. It is in the cosmic that our yoke becomes easy and our burden light; it is in the cosmic that we find the love that abideth forever, the power that cannot be measured, the truth that gives freedom to body, mind and soul, the wisdom that is luminous as the light of the eternal sun; and we shall enter the splendor of the cosmic when we begin to live ON THE HEIGHTS.

When we enter the cosmic we find the real sweetness of existence; the ills and imperfections of life have vanished; the mind can know no evil, the body can feel no pain. We are far beyond the clouds of doubt and fear, because we are in that world where everything is true and everything is good. We are under the clear sky of Infinite Light, on the verge of the great beyond, on the borderland of the limitless, on the shores of the great eternal sea; we have found the heaven of perfect bliss, and every moment is an eternity of ecstasy divine.

When we have been within the pearly gates of the cosmic world, even but for a moment, life is not the same any more; life is no longer mere existence but a sacred something that we hold too precious to even mention in spoken words. It is beyond words, and beyond thought, too great, too marvelous, too wondrously beautiful for mind to fathom or tongue describe. The soul alone can know such a life, and after we have tasted the fruits of the cosmic, the meat that we know not of, nothing less than such a life can satisfy.

The personal man may feel contented to exist in the valley of mere things, but not so with the awakened soul. The soul that is awakened must live on the mountain tops of the spirit; the joy of the soul is ON THE HEIGHTS, and we give the soul its greatest ecstasy when we mount upon the wings of spirit and soar to empyrian heights.

TO LIVE ON THE HEIGHTS is to enter into the realization and the conscious possession of the best that life can give, not only on the spiritual plane, but on all planes; and the higher we ascend towards the greater heights the more we shall receive of everything that is rich and beautiful in human existence made divine.

The life sublime is therefore the life of the greatest good to the entire being of man—body, mind and soul. It means health, wholeness and purity for the body, wisdom, power and illumination for the mind, and the glories of the cosmic realm for the soul.

When we live ON THE HEIGHTS the body is filled with the wholeness of the spirit, the mind is inspired with power from on high, while the soul is basking eternally in the sunshine of Infinite Love. Every impulse of life is music from enchanted realms, and every thought is an angel, radiant with loveliness and joy. And this is life—the most beautiful gift of God.

To ascend to the heights is to reach that coveted goal where the ideal is made real, where every dream comes true and where every vision of the soul is transformed into that tangible something we have wished for so long. The supreme heights do not simply present us with the mental picture of that which we long to receive; when we reach the heights we receive the substance of things hoped for and the evidence of things not seen. We receive upon earth what we hoped to find in heaven.

In the cosmic world the ideal is real and the real is ideal. Therefore, to ascend to the heights is to find that our ideals are not mere pictures, but realities—substantial things of a higher order—the product of workmanship divine. And these sublime realities are so constituted that they can be made tangible parts of daily personal life. This is the Word becoming flesh, the life of the soul unfolded into the beauty and the charm of exalted personal expression.

To heal the body and emancipate the mind, the secret is to ascend to the heights. In those lofty realms no ill can come to man, neither can the turmoil of the world affect him anymore. Whatever his outer conditions may be, he remains untouched, unmoved and undisturbed. He is living in that beautiful calm "where dwells the soul serene," and all is silent and still. And out of that silence comes the symphony of life, the tender tones of heaven-born music taking him away to those enchanted realms where life itself is an endless song.

To feel the touch of the silence of the soul is to fully understand those inspired words, "Let not your heart be troubled"; there is a place prepared for us where troubles can never enter, where pains are forever barred. This sacred place is the heaven within, and it is the will of the Most High that we should enter now while still in personal form.

When we live ON THE HEIGHTS we realize that we live and move and have our being in a great divine sea. We feel that we are fully surrounded by the essence of pure spirit, and we can touch God everywhere. We are in a world that is luminous with spiritual light, and we can see clearly the meaning of everything. Nothing is mysterious any more; our minds are full of light; and we know the truth, and this truth has made us free.

We also realize that we are in a world of higher power, and we can feel that power working with us whenever we wish it so to be. This power is limitless, and here we find ' the secret why those who live ON THE HEIGHTS can never fail.

They are carried on and on to victory whatever conditions may be. Obstacles that seem insurmountable vanish in a night, enemies are changed into the most worthy of friends, and on the very eve when all seems lost, the elements are transformed, the tide turns, fate is conquered, and the battle is won.

There is nothing to fear when we live ON THE HEIGHTS, because we may call upon the power of the Supreme, and this power cannot fail. It will take us safely through the most difficult and the most adverse of conditions, and transform the saddest states of existence into a world of comfort and joy.

When we are ON THE HEIGHTS we can feel this power; we can feel that it is moving, changing and transforming everything, causing all things to go with us to the goal we have in view. And though it may seem to be a power not our own, nevertheless, it is our own, because all that the Father hath is mine.

The secret of all great and lofty souls is found in this higher power; they have ascended to the heights, they are living on the mountain tops of the spirit, and God is with them. They have found that supreme world where my Father worketh and I work, and whatever they may undertake to do the same shall be done. Nothing can stand in their way; what works against them is mysteriously changed, and proceeds with heart and soul to work for them. Their plans for greater things are worked out in a wonderful manner; their lofty aims are realized and their dearest desires fulfilled. Their secret is simple; they are living ON THE HEIGHTS, and the limitless power of the Infinite is with them.

WHEN we live ON THE HEIGHTS we wait eternally upon the Lord, and they that wait upon the Lord shall renew their strength. Neither weariness nor weakness are possible because in the cosmic world we are one with God and to be one with God is to be filled, through and through, with the limitless power of God.

To wait upon the Lord is to give ourselves completely to the Most High; it is to live for the Infinite and when we live for the Infinite, the Infinite will live in us. The power of the Almighty will be given as freely as we can possibly receive, and therefore our strength will ever be renewed.

The limitations of the person will pass away, and whatever we may be called upon to do, we shall receive strength and power in abundance from above. All things will become possible because God is with us, and God is with us because we are with God.

When we choose to go with God, then He will go with us, and we always choose to go with Him when we ascend to the heights. To live in the realms of the life sublime is to live as God lives, and to live as God lives is to be one with God—to live and move and have our being in Him —to feel that His presence is closer than breathing, nearer than hands and feet.

To live ON THE HEIGHTS is to enter into that divine relationship where we know that My Father and I are one. It is in this state that we behold the face of the Infinite, where we awaken to the great truth that His countenance is beautiful—altogether lovely—the fairest of ten thousand to the soul.

And we are created in His image and likeness, heirs to His Kingdom, destined to live an eternity with Him —destined to manifest the same loveliness, the same perfection, the same divinity, the same supreme joy. Beautiful thought, thought of sweetness and peace! The mere thinking of this thought will inspire the soul to feel the divinity of its own exalted existence and ascend to those heights where the light of His glory is shining forever.

When those gentle moments creep o'er us—those moments that awaken the tender sweetness of life, we long to be with God, we long to feel His presence, and nothing else can satisfy; the soul is calling for its own, waiting and yearning to be taken in the arms of Infinite Love; and those moments are sacred indeed. The soul is awakened; it is on the verge of another and a better world; we are upon holy ground and should lift our hearts in worship as we never worshiped before; we are about to be born again, to be born of the spirit, to be taken in the arms of love to His secret places on high.

Whenever the soul begins to yearn for the Infinite, the divinity within us is awakened, and we are ready to ascend to the heights, we **are** ready for a better world, and it is our privilege to enter that better world, even now, while still in personal form. The joys of heaven are for the present —the endless present, and the soul that lives ON THE HEIGHTS may inherit those joys to-day.

The secret path that leads to the heights may be found in the stillness of the soul. To meet the Infinite we must enter the silent within, and when we enter into His presence we are lifted at once to the heights. To be with Him is to be ON THE HEIGHTS, and the beautiful within is the gates ajar to His Kingdom.

The sacred stillness of the beautiful within no tongue can ever describe; it is one of those secret places of which we are not permitted to speak, because it is beyond the power of speech. To know the within we must enter the within, and faith is the open door—the faith that is born of the spirit—the faith we feel when we are touched by the spirit.

The true spiritual faith knows; it knows because it is animated by the spirit, inspired by the spirit, illumined by the spirit; it knows the way, it knows the truth, it knows the life; therefore if we follow this faith we shall find what we seek; we shall enter the beautiful within and ascend to the glories of the spiritual heights.

To follow the ascending light of the true spiritual faith is to keep the eye single upon the great eternal light, and so long as we see that light and that light alone we shall pass upward and onward eternally towards the greatest heights of God's transcendent worlds. We shall turn neither to the left nor to the right, because our minds will be filled with the one light, and that light alone will guide us. Thus we shall follow the straight and narrow path—the path that leads into life—the limitless life of the beautiful cosmic world.

To enter into the realization of that life is to live from above, to have eternal being in the lofty realms of the spirit, to be safely fixed on high; and to be fixed on high is the secret of that unbounded spiritual strength that gives the ascended soul its great invincible power. The soul that has gained this power has entered into possession of supreme spiritual mastery; such a soul may truthfully and eternally declare, "None of these things move me any more. God is my strength and my power, and His Will alone shall remain."

HERE is nothing in the world that will not change, and change most beautifully when we begin to live ON THE HEIGHTS. That which is not good disappears completely, while that which is good becomes infinitely better. And the secret of this change is found in the realization of one of the most inspiring truths that the human mind can ever know.

When we ascend to the heights we meet the smile of God, and "how soon a smile of God can change the world." The elements of life are illumined with the radiance of His glory, and the tenderness of His loving smile inspires everything to be good, beautiful and kind.   We are transported, body, mind and soul, into a new world, and how good it is to be there.

We can see the smile of God in everything; all things become mirrors, reflecting the joyousness and the sweetness of the smile from on high. Darkness changes into light, pain changes into pleasure, tribulation changes into peace, adversity changes into love, and life becomes an endless song.   Wherever we go we radiate the smile of God, and all things reciprocate by smiling in return.

A great change has come over us, and everybody can see it.   We are no longer mere humans, nor do we dwell in the valley any more; we are living ON THE HEIGHTS and we belong to a higher, finer world. There is something in our nature, our countenance and our speech that inspires others to be happy; we bring sunshine wherever we go, and to be with us is a joy that cannot be measured.

To serve us in every conceivable manner is counted a rare privilege by everybody; we are giving so much to the world, and the world gains pleasure from giving us much in return. Nothing is too good for us, we are everywhere in demand and a royal welcome is everywhere in store. Our friends are as legions and the thoughts of love that we daily receive are as numberless as the sands of the shore.

We have found the great secret; we have been ON THE HEIGHTS; we have seen the smile of God, and how soon that smile has changed our world. Where we saw neither hope nor opportunity we can now see both in abundance. We have more opportunities than we can take advantage of and our hopes are becoming realizations, richer by far than we ever expected. We are living a charmed life and everything we touch turns to happiness.

The world about us everywhere reflects the glory of our own joy; we can see so clearly the good and the beautiful in everything, and all things seem to make a special effort to present to us their most beautiful side only. Even the clouds turn about so we may see nothing but the silver lining, and pain cries aloud, declaring it only means to be pleasure whenever we appear on the scene.

The secret of it all is simply this, we carry with us the smile of God, and how soon that smile can change the world. When we see that smile we learn how we are made for happiness, because God is supreme happiness, and we are created in His image and likeness. So great is the joy of the Infinite that to simply touch the hem of His garment· is to feel a million thrills of sublime ecstasy.

TO LOVE everybody with the dearest, the purest and the highest love of the soul becomes a part of life itself when we live in the smile of God. This smile inspires real, heart-felt love for everything because it comes from Him who is love. All things were created in the spirit of love and by the power of love, therefore to love everything becomes one of the exquisite delights of the soul when we live in Him whose very life is love.

The smile of God is the smile of gentleness, tenderness and kindness; and when we carry this smile with us, we shall always be kind. Every thought we think will be a benediction, every word we speak will give peace and harmony to life, and everything we do will add to the comfort and happiness of man. To give our very best to the world will be our dearest desire, and our gifts will be precious indeed, because whatever we give, we give also the smile of God.

The more we smile with the smile of God, and the more we live and give in the spirit of this smile, the more abundantly will life be enriched with the treasures of sublime existence. We gain happiness from every source in the world—the visible world and the cosmic world, because the smile of God not only is happiness but it awakens everything that can produce happiness.

When we live in that smile every

movement is a pleasure, every thought is a dancing sunbeam of joy, and every impulse is a revelation of some fair enchanted realm. It is then that work becomes play because all our duties are set to the music of the spheres. The elements of life glide merrily and merrily on as if charmed by the magic touch of some strange enraptured power. And it is true; all things within us and about us are charmed; we are living in a charmed world—charmed with the smile of God.

The forces of adversity, with all their displeasing conditions, can enter our world no more; we are living ON THE HEIGHTS in the smile of God, and where God is smiling, there we shall find neither sorrow nor trouble nor pain. When we ascend to the heights we find healing for the body, emancipation for the mind and inspiration for the soul. We are in God's own beautiful world, and how good it is to be there.

Whatever our conditions may be in personal life, there are better things in store. When things are wrong we simply ascend to the heights and all is well again. ON THE HEIGHTS we meet the smile of God, and how soon that smile can change the world. That which is imperfect passes away as darkness before the glory of the rising sun, and the real beauty of life is revealed in all its lovliness divine.

When we ascend to the heights we find that the richness and splendor of life is not simply beautiful in the highest terms of sense, but that it is gorgeous — indescribably gorgeous, and that the sublimity of its grandeur far transcends our most exalted dreams of the celestial city on high. "Eye hath not seen nor ear heard, neither hath it entered into the heart of man what God has prepared for them that love Him." The understanding of the personal man cannot discern these things, but the awakened soul ascends to the heights, and beholds what sublime existence has in store.

And it is then that the soul learns to know that God is love, that His goodness abideth forever, and that His kindness is as limitless as the Infinite sea. Everything is given to man.   Nothing is withheld.   All that the Father hath is mine.   It is His will and His good pleasure to give us the Kingdom, but to receive the Kingdom we must go to Him.   We must go and live in God's world, and God's world is ON THE HEIGHTS.

In the silence of the spirit,
In the higher realms above,
In the deeper life within me,
In the world of perfect love,
I have found my Father's kingdom
And his righteousness divine;
I have sought and found my heaven,
And all else is ever mine.

From this higher life within me,
I shall nevermore depart,
Living ever in the spirit,
Seeking Truth with all my heart;
Drawing nearer, ever nearer,
To the Source of life sublime,
Ever rising higher, higher,
Through the endlessness of time.

Steps To The Heights

WHEN we proceed to ascend to the mountain tops of the spirit, we find a number of steps leading to those sublime heights, and if we follow those steps as they appear in succession upon the rising pathway of life, we shall surely reach our lofty goal. But we must observe that the steps are many, that they are all necessary parts of the path, and that each step must be taken as it appears before us whether it appears in the same manner to-day as yesterday, or not. All of those steps are met many times on the upward path; sometimes they appear in one order, sometimes in another, because there must be no monotony in the ascending life, and all the elements of the soul must be unfolded in actual expression.

1. Give your best to the world, and give in greater and greater abundance, regardless of what the world may give to you. This giving will awaken the soul, because everything that is to be given must come from the soul, and the more the soul is called upon to come forth with its precious treasures, the more will the soul *live* in the unfoldment of the richness of its divine life. The soul that gives much becomes much; it gives expression to much, and through this expression unfolds every element of divine being. The beauty of the

spiritual life comes forth, the soul is awakened, and it is only the awakened soul that can ascend to the heights. But this giving must come from the heart; it must be the giving of love, for love gives because it loves to give, and for no other reason whatever.

2. Live in the world of the good, the true and the beautiful, and think on these things. Whatever is lovely, beautiful, perfect, lofty and sublime, let the mind dwell with these things, and let the mind choose such alone for its ceaseless companions. The mind becomes like its constant companions, and it is only the mind that is true and good and beautiful that can ascend to the heights. The mind that would ascend to the heights must "think beautiful thoughts and send

them adrift on eternity's boundless sea", and must surround itself completely with a mighty host of angels—good thoughts, created in the image and likeness of Infinite thought. The ascending soul thinks God's thoughts after Him, and it is upon the wings of such thoughts that the soul is carried to the shining glory of the cosmic realm.

3. Know that you are a spiritual being, and that you live and move and have your being in an infinite sea of pure celestial spirit. Know that you are surrounded, here and now, by the radiant elements of the cosmic world, and in that sublime realization, live, think and act eternally. To give constant recognition to the spirit in which you live is to place the elements

of your life in closer and closer touch with the spirit. Thus your body, mind and soul will be spiritualized more and more, the material elements of your being will be removed from your senses and your visions, and your eyes will be opened to the splendor of "another and a better world."

4. Live in the constant recognition of the great truth that God is with you, that He is nearer than your very life, because He is the very Life of your life. Keep this thought before the mind always and draw so near to His nearness that you can *feel* the glory of His divine presence. This will awaken your own spiritual nature which means that you will begin to live with God and walk with God; and those who are

walking with God are on the heights because God is always on the heights.

5. Keep the eye single upon the light of the great eternal sun, and open your mind to the endless influx of that light. Thus you become full of the light, you will actually live in a sea of light, and to live *in* the light is to be on the heights. When the mind is illumined with light from above, all the elements of mind and soul will turn towards that light as the flower turns her smiling face towards the light of the sun; and when the soul turns towards the Infinite light, it will begin to ascend, drawing nearer and nearer to that light. In like manner, all the elements of human life will begin to look up, and that which is looking up will rise. Body, mind and soul will

begin to ascend, and, in harmony, will shortly reach the lofty goal.

6. Live in the spiritual understanding of the truth. Open the mind to the truth as it is in all things, and know that every creature in the universe manifests truth in its own individual measure. Recognize the truth as the source of all orderly expression, and live perpetually in that consciousness that discerns the reality of absolute truth—the truth as it is in the Mind of God. Thus will your own mind find its true state of being, its true relation to God, to man, to all that is; the mind will be true to itself, it will be truth in itself, it will know that it is, within the reality of itself, the divine perfection of truth. This truth will make the

mind free, and when the mind is free the soul ascends to the heights. To know the truth is to live on the heights where all things are created in the beautiful likeness of the Infinite.

7. Dwell eternally in the highest spiritual touch with the divinity that is in every living creature. Live only with the divine, think only of the divine, look only for the divine, and know that the divine is everywhere. On the heights everything is divinity in expression, and only those can ascend to the heights that recognize the divine that lives in every form of expression. To consciously recognize the divine in all things, and live in spiritual touch with the divine everywhere, the mind must live in

that attitude where boundless love is wedded to that realization that knows the spiritual nature of all things. Think of all things as they are in the perfection of divine spirit, and in that thought love all things with the infinite tenderness of boundless love.

8. Merge yourself with the universal. Come out from the cramped world of limitation and enter the freedom of the limitless. There are no limitations on the heights; we must therefore eliminate every thought of limitation before we can ascend to the heights. The mountain tops of the spirit are in the sublime world of the boundless, where the soul is free to stretch forth its wings and soar wherever it will. There is

nothing in the way; everything is is free to be all that it is, and in being all, it unfolds the universal, the limitless, the endless, thus living what it is—the likeness of God.

9. Live by that faith that is ever on the verge of the great beyond—the infinite sea of unbounded life; the faith that knows that the unseen is real, that the seeming void is solid rock, that the great beyond is a more marvelous universe inseparably united with that which seems real now. This faith knows that all is real, that God is everywhere, that the soul may press on into the vastness of limitless worlds and still be ever in the presence of the Most High. This faith removes the veil that seems to separate the world of sense from the

universal sea of spirit; it reveals to the mind the great truth that all worlds, visible and invisible, are one world, and in this one world may be found the many mansions of the soul. This faith takes the soul out of the material into the spiritual and when the soul awakens to the spiritual it begins to ascend to the heights.

10. Dwell constantly in a high spiritual touch with the master minds of the ages. Feel that you are one with these in the spirit and that by virtue of that oneness, the secret of their sublime existence is also being revealed to you. Nourish the mind constantly with the inspired thoughts of these great souls, thus preparing the mind to realize and express in real life, the same oneness that already

exists in spirit. Live, in spirit, with the Christ, and the true spiritual followers of the Christ, in whatever times or places these may be found. Let these be the constant companions of the soul, for they constitute the great white throng that is living on the heights. Whether they be in the form or not, if they are in the spirit they are on the heights, and to live in spiritual touch with such exalted souls is to ascend to the heights.

11. Pray without ceasing, and pray with all the power of heart and soul, that you may ascend into God's own beautiful world. Ceaselessly desire the highest, and inspire every thought with the soul of this desire. The action of every desire, whether of the body, mind or soul, should be

animated with a strong ascending life. The whole of life should be made a prayer—a beautiful prayer of faith—a prayer for the spiritual life on high. And whatsoever we desire, pray for, or ask for, we should ask it in the name of the Christ; not simply in the verbal expression of that name, but in the spiritual understanding of that name. To enter the spiritual understanding of the name of the Christ when we pray is to enter into that spiritual world where everything that we may pray for is already at hand for us to receive. Whatsoever ye pray or ask for, believe that ye have received it and ye shall have it. It has already been given; it is already at hand in the kingdom waiting for us to come and take possession; and I Am the door; we may enter the kingdom and receive our own providing we enter in the name of the Christ, in the pure spiritual conception' of the divine significance of that name.

12. Thy will be done. To place the whole of life in the power of Infinite Will, is to go *with* this will, and the Will of God always wills to go to the highest. The Infinite Will is ever ascending, therefore when we choose to accept this Will as our will, we shall also ascend. When we will to do what God wills, we shall go and live in His own beautiful world, because that is His Will. It is His Will that all should enter His Kingdom now, and His Kingdom is ON THE HEIGHTS.

My life is filled with wisdom,
With power and with love;
The light of truth is shining
With splendor from above.
My path is strewn with roses,
My sky is bright and clear;
My heart is filled with virtue,
And boundless good is near.

My life is filled with glory,
With happiness and peace;
I'm free from pain and darkness,
From sorrow and disease.
I live the life of spirit,
The life of love divine;
The sweetness of existence
Is now forever mine.

The Soul's Prayer

Infinite Father, Eternal Spirit, Omnipresent Divinity, the highest love of my heart and soul is for thee.

Thou art all that is beautiful, all that is good, all that is true, all that is divine.

From eternity to eternity my life is in thee, and thy house of the many mansions, my everlasting home.

I behold thy shining countenance, radiant with loveliness and infinite joy. I feel thy omnipresence, and know that thou art closer than breathing, nearer than hands and feet.

Thy infinite love is in my heart, going forth to all the world, an angel of peace, kindness and sympathy. Thy goodness fills me and surrounds me. In thee everything is good. I live in thee and all is good in me.

Thou art perfect being, and I am thy image and likeness. Thou art eternal, without beginning and without end, and as thou art, the same am I also.

I have always lived in thee, and in thee I shall live eternally; beautiful, endless existence divine.

Infinite Father, God of all that is beautiful and true, I am one with thee. We are united forever in all that is, for thou livest in me and I in thee.

Thou art perfection, and I am thy image and likeness. Thou art divine wholeness, and as thou art, I am, for in all things I am thy likeness divine.

I am perfect and whole in body; I am pure and clean in mind; I am strong and beautiful in soul, for I am thy image and likeness.

I am walking with thee; wherever I go thou art always with me; therefore my ways are ways of pleasantness and all my paths are peace.

The shining glory of thy kingdom is ever before me; in the light of thy radiant countenance do I dwell forever. Every moment of my existence is an eternity of bliss, and I rejoice everlastingly while my heart is singing with countless angel throngs.

Thy beautiful children, the numberless souls of thy omnipresent kingdom, are all with me; they are my eternal companions, their faces beaming with infinite joy, their garments shining with the glory and splendor of thy luminous presence.

Wherever my body may be, wherever my mind may roam, I am always in thee, living in thy beautiful heaven, abiding forever in thy arms of tenderness and love.

Thy spirit ever leads me through the endless pathways of life's delightful journey, and all that is good is ever coming to me. Thou art my safety, my guide and my protection, and all is well.

592734 A

I shall be taught of thee all that I needs must know at every step of the perfect way. The light of thy wisdom shall ever shine upon me, and I shall think thy thoughts after thee.

Infinite Father, Supreme Creator of all the world, thou art my life and my power; thou art my wisdom and my understanding; thou art my tenderness and my love; thou art my peace and my joy; thou art my purity and my wholeness; thou art my virtue and my supply. From thee do I ever receive all that eternal life can give, the boundlessness of thy infinite kingdom.

In thee there is wisdom and light; in thee there is power and love; in thee there is glory and joy; in thee there is wholeness and strength; in thee there is virtue and peace; in thee there is freedom and life; in thee there is goodness and truth; in thee there is all that was, is or evermore shall be, and in thee I live and move and have my being.

Thou livest in me, and I in thee; and all that is in thee is in me, for I am thy image and likeness.

My heart is filled with tenderness and love for all the world; every soul in existence is dear to me, for we are all thy children, forever living in thee, filled and surrounded with thy tender love and care. And before me all is beautiful and all is well.

Infinite Father, to know thee is to dwell eternally in the secret places of the Most High, in the highest heavens, upon those supreme heights where thy infinite glory is shining forever.

And thou hast revealed thyself to me; I have learned to know thee face to face; I am even now in thy beautiful presence, and before me lies the endless pathway of the life eternal; upward and onward forever, ever ascending into greater and greater glory, ever drawing nearer and nearer to the omnipresent throne of God.

Infinite Father, I am forever with thee, and how good it is to be here; before me all is beautiful, my very pathway glittering with celestial brilliancy in the heavenly light of the eternal sun.

This is life, and I thank thee; with all my heart and soul I thank thee forever and ever, for thou art goodness eternal, kindness and love divine.

Thus shall I ever live; filled and surrounded with God; walking hand in hand with the great white throng; abiding in the kingdom; living in the great eternal light; giving to all the world the boundlessness of the gifts of love from on high; dwelling eternally upon the sublime heights of divine existence, the shining mountain tops of the spirit, and ever ascending to the greater glories prepared for me in my Father's House.

Onward, souls eternal,
Rise and walk with God;
Come and tread the pathway
That the saints have trod;
Ever upward, onward,
Soar to heights sublime,
Live on spirit's mountain
All the days of time.

Onward, souls eternal,
Rise in spirit's might,
Rise to realms supernal,
Realms of endless light;
Live the life of spirit,
Perfect life divine,
Live where God's great glory
Evermore shall shine.

Onward, souls eternal,
Sons of God to be;
Rise to endless glory,
Power and majesty.

Lightning Source UK Ltd.
Milton Keynes UK
UKHW02f2007200818
327529UK00009B/285/P